EAGER EVERLY

VOLUME 2: MY FIRST CAR RIDE

Prelude

Hi, My name is Everly Irene and
I'm eager to try new things.
Join me in my journey through life,
as I grow, learn, and play.
Let the fun begin!

I am on a new adventure.
Family time on the road.
Inside the car we snuggle up,
As we head to our comfy home.

The car ride is so smooth,
That mommy falls asleep.
But me, I am wide awake,
Taking in lights, signs, and beeps.
BEEP!
BEEEEEEEPP

I must be very special,
Or at least, that's what I think.
Because I am the only one,
Facing backwards in my seat.

I see the pretty colors,
Like red, yellow, and green.
They must also be pretty special,
Because they're on every street I see.

Artist - some song number 1
Artist - some song number 2
Artist - some song number 3
Artist - some song number 4

Slow and fast and twist and turn,
Our journey is almost done.
But I am not in any rush,
Because I am having fun.

I think the ride is over,
Because the car has stopped.
Dad turns around and says,
"It's time to hop on out."

Mommy grabs my blanket,
And cuddles me real tight.
Into the house we go,
After my first car ride.

Cars come in many different shapes and sizes.
Some cars are red or green, and others have fun surprises.
Riding with a loved one can always be a hoot.
Especially when you're with the ones you love,
You'll make fond memories too!

What day did we go home after I was born? (day, month, year, time of day)

____

____

Describe the day we went home? (weather, sights, sounds, smells)

____

____

How did you feel on our first car ride together?

____

____

What was I doing during my first car ride?

____

____

For Everly Irene Grace

Written by John William Grace Jr.
Edited by Daniella Grace

www.ingramcontent.com/pod-product-compliance
Lightning Source LLC
Chambersburg PA
CBRC090749110726
48005CB00008B/1022